The Vegie Patch

A storytelling book about the familiar hobby of gardening. The story follows the months of growing home vegetables and takes the viewer from the building of the vegetable patch to planting, caring, reaping and cooking the vegetables.

The book is an interactive activity for a carer or therapist to share with a care-recipient in one-on-one situations or as a group activity. It is designed for people with Alzheimer's disease, dementia, memory loss and frail aged persons. The images are intended to facilitate social identity and memory stimulation through recognition of the familiar, cuing and some repetition. The book may be used in conjunction with *The Vegetable Patch* movie to support reminiscence and recognition.

Carers' Viewing Suggestions:

- Sit beside your care-recipient in a non-invasive position, express your interest & respond to care-recipient's engagement.
- View the book with your care-recipient in a quiet area with no distracting noises or activities nearby.
- Make sure there are no bright lights or bright windows to the viewer's side or in front, as these will be distracting.
- Make sure there are no shadows or reflecting lights falling on the pages.
- Provide focus by avoiding distracting patterns within the viewing area. If sitting at a table place a plain cloth (not bright, fluro or white) over fabric patterns, clutter or other activity resources.
- Provide a plain covered pillow or cushion on your care-recipient's lap to support their hands and the book.
- Check that care-recipients glasses are clean.
- Where possible allow your care-recipient control of turning the pages and pausing for engagement and reminiscence.
- Make a note of interesting stories or memories that your reader has talked about or images that attracted attention for future interaction.
- A sigh, nod, smile or other non-verbal expression may be considered as social interaction for some persons in care.

www.sharetimepictures.com.au

Photography & Design: Judi Parkinson B.V.A, F.A., B.A. (Psychology), M.A. (Hons) V.A.

Copyright © Judi Parkinson 2013 All rights reserved

No part of this publication may be reproduced or copied by any person or organisation via any media including all mechanical, photographic and electronic means. Permission for reproduction or photocopying of any part of the contents is not granted and doing so is in breach of copyright laws unless prior written permission from the copyright owner has been given.

Parkinson, Judi, 1948-
The Vegie Patch - A Share-Time Picture Book for Reminiscing and Storytelling
Publisher: Brisbane, Judi Parkinson for Share-Time Pictures, Amazon Edition 2014
ISBN-13: 978-1497333000 ISBN-10: 1497333008
Series: Non-Verbal Reminiscent Books for People with Alzheimer's disease, Dementia and Memory Loss - Volume 4.

Made in the USA
Coppell, TX
04 December 2021